I Wrote This Book on Purpose...

So You Can Know Yours

Dr. John W. Stanko

Evergreen
PRESS

Evergreen Press
P.O. Box 191540 • Mobile, AL 36619
(800) 367-8203
www.evergreenpressbooks.com
info@evergreen777.com

ISBN 1-58169-011-8
For Worldwide Distribution
Printed in the U.S.A.

TABLE OF CONTENTS

DEDICATION

To my only sister, Janet Folino,
whose purpose has led her to serve others
and our family for many years.
Thank you, Janet, for investing your life
for the wellbeing of others.

FOREWORD

I am happy to write these few words of introduction for my friend of many years, Dr. John Stanko. John's book on purpose is powerful, yet entertaining. John is one of the clearest communicators I have ever heard, and the truth he communicates in these pages can change your life. I can say this because understanding purpose and applying it practically to life has been one of my goals in life. I believe this book to be the key to a happy, healthy and successful life. These truths will not only improve your personal and spiritual world, but also your financial world. As God comes through these pages to your mind and out into your life, you will see why I appreciated the principles found in this book. For a number of years, John has been certified through the Institute for Motivational Living, and we not only apply this system in our own Institute, but we have personally profited from these truths. You are in for a real treat!

Dr. Sanford Gerald Kulkin
President, Institute for Motivational Living

INTRODUCTION

*To have a great purpose to work for, a purpose
larger than ourselves, is one of the secrets of
making life significant, for then the meaning and
worth of the individual overflow his personal
borders and survive his death.*
       —Will Durant

It all began in November 1991. I was visiting a
Nazarene church in Pismo Beach, California, and for the
first time, I was going to teach my seminar entitled,
"Effectiveness: Functioning in Your Purpose." The con-
text was a "Come and Worship!" event sponsored by
Worship International, the ministry division of Integrity
Music.

I was apprehensive, to say the least, as I waited for
the session to begin. I rehearsed again in my mind all the
objections I had raised when the director, Steve
Bowersox, suggested we offer the class on an experi-
mental basis. "These are musicians and song leaders," I
told Steve, "and they won't be interested in what I have to
say. They want technical and musical help and aren't
looking for a philosophical discussion on life purpose."

But Steve firmly insisted, so I stood at the podium, waiting to see if anyone would come.

To my surprise and relief, people *did* come. To my greater surprise and relief, so did the Lord. I sensed His favor as I taught the principles of purpose that had become so pertinent in my life. As I taught, I noticed that a number of people were deeply moved and even wept during parts of my presentation. The 75 minutes went quickly, and people gathered around to ask me questions and to express appreciation. Steve was right: if I taught it, they would come.

People continued to come to that class for the next five years as I offered it at every "Come and Worship!" weekend. My purpose class was consistently one of the most popular classes on our seminar evaluations. When we went "international," I had the chance to present the class in Malaysia, Singapore, Hong Kong, Taiwan, England, and other countries.

The results were always the same: people were deeply touched and affected. I have received many testimonial letters from people who made radical life-direction changes as a result of what they heard in my class. Later, I expanded the session into an all-day seminar, and thousands have come to learn how to identify and engage their life's purpose. In addition, I wrote my first book, *Life is a Gold Mine: Can You Dig It?*, to respond to the demand for more material to study after attending the seminar. *Life Is a Gold Mine* has sold thousands of copies and is currently being translated for distribution in China and India. After my affiliation with Worship International came to an end, I have continued to visit churches to conduct weekend seminars. The presentation that began in 1991 is featured in an audio tape entitled, *I Recorded This Tape on Purpose*. (See page 82 for ordering information.)

I've never had anyone challenge me as to the validity, worth or biblical correctness of my purpose presentation. Most everyone knows the truth about purpose intuitively. Most people who are familiar with the Bible have at one time or another quoted to someone the words of Romans 8:28: *"All things work together for good for those who love God and are called according to His* purpose*"* (emphasis added).

But many have found that talking about purpose is much easier than defining it in a personal way. I wrote this book on purpose to help you get beyond the first step of agreeing that you have a purpose, so that you can clearly identify the reason you were born. And I'm more convinced than ever before that it's possible for everyone to do that, including you!

In my travels and research, I've met many wonderful people who have the same burden that I do: to see people doing not just *good* things, but the *best* things that they were created to do. I've also found that other groups— with differing philosophical perspectives—have pursued this issue and have produced some interesting books and articles on the topic. For instance, Laurence G. Boldt wrote these words in his book, *How to Find the Work You Love:*

The quest for the work you love—it all begins with the two simple questions: "Who am I?" and "What in the world am I doing here?" While as old as humanity itself, these perennial questions are born anew in every man and woman who is privileged to walk upon this earth. Every sane man and woman, at some point in his or her life, is confronted by these questions—some while but children; more in adolescence and youth; still more at midlife or when facing retirement; and even the toughest customers at the death of a loved one or when they themselves have a brush with death. Yes, somewhere, sometime, we all find ourselves face to face with the questions, "Who am I?" and "What am I here for?"

And we do make some attempt to answer them. We ask our parents and teachers, and it seems they do not know. They refer us to political and religious institutions, which often crank out canned answers devoid of personal meaning. Some even tell us that life has no meaning, save for eating and breeding. Most of us are smart enough to recognize that canned answers or begging the question will not do. We must find real answers for ourselves. But that takes more heart and effort than we are often willing to give.

I agree with much of what Mr. Boldt wrote. I can confirm from my experience that almost everyone faces the issue of purpose at one time or another. You are also, or you probably wouldn't be reading this book or trying to answer the questions, "Who am I?" and "What am I here for?" People begin their quest for answers at different stages of life, some in childhood and some at retirement.

Furthermore, religious institutions sometimes offer "canned answers" that leave people with simplistic solutions to those tough questions. Often people tell me that they are here "to do the will of God," "glorify God," "serve others," or "worship Him." But these answers stop short, for you must go further to find the specific will of God for your life: what it is that will glorify God, how you can serve others, and what it means to worship God beyond singing a hymn or chorus on Sunday morning.

The pursuit of answers "takes more heart and effort than we are often willing to give," as Mr. Boldt wrote. It's so much easier to settle for pat answers or to have someone else define who you are. But that's like putting a band-aid on a major laceration: it may look good and even cover the wound, but it won't necessarily bring the desired long-term results, clarity or fulfillment.

I do take issue with Mr. Boldt, however, as to the source of the insight and revelation necessary to answer the questions raised. Mr. Boldt also wrote a book entitled *Zen and the Art of Making a Living*. The answer for him can come from many sources, since Zen promotes the total enlightenment of an individual through meditation and work. The answers for my questions do not come from self-enlightenment or consulting a guru; my answers come from Him who created me and assigned me a purpose according to His will.

It isn't uncommon for those who discuss the topic of purpose, at some point, to refer to the issue of a life's calling or vocation. The word *vocation* comes from the Latin word *vocare,* which means to call. In the original use of the word, a person could be called or have the vocation of a shoemaker. Eventually, having a vocation or call became associated with a religious calling to the priesthood or some other form of ministry.

The very concept of a calling means that there is some intelligent force doing the calling. I cannot conceive of how an activity can call out to a person. A calling presupposes an intelligent being, force, or person is doing the calling. A calling comes *from* someone— God—*to* someone—His created (see Appendix I).

It is when I seek to serve God and cooperate with His plan that I have found my life to have meaning and direction. As the psalmist wrote, *"My help comes from the Lord, the maker of heaven and earth"* (Psalm 121:2). The designer of anything is the perfect one to define the purpose of the designed, and that is why I look to—even expect—the God of heaven and earth to answer my purpose questions. Mr. Boldt writes:

> Finding the work you love is not a cerebral process. It is not a matter of figuring something out through a process of rational analysis. It is a process of opening yourself and beginning to pay attention to what you respond to with energy and enthusiasm. Pay attention to the people,

events, and activities in the outside world that evoke the strongest response from you. Pay attention as well to your inside world, to the inspirations and intuitions that most excite you. From within and without, let yourself be moved. Listen to your own heart and learn to trust what it is saying.

My desire is to help you listen and be moved from without and within. With that in mind, this book is a combination workbook and inspirational reader. I want you to be further inspired and directed through a collection of quotes, personal testimonies, and real-life stories that I've collected over the last seven years. But I also want you to be equipped with greater understanding of the whole topic of purpose, and so I have included some further insights not found in *Life Is a Gold Mine*. We'll also take a look at some case studies of biblical and historical figures that were successful because they were men and women of purpose. In addition, a bibliography of other material is included that will be helpful for further study.

I've left wide margins in this book for a reason: I want you to *write* in them. Record your thoughts or impressions as you read, or jot down cross references that you want to look up later. As you set your mind and heart to seek your purpose, it's important to pay attention to the thoughts and impressions that are calling you. They may not even make sense right now, but it's important that you "honor" them as they come. If you've never written in your books before, it's critical that you write in this one.

The last seven years have been the most fulfilling of my life. I've been focused on my own purpose, and I've seen so many people come to a better understanding of who they are and why they're here. But much work remains to be done. I wrote this book on purpose to further the quest in every person to find the reason they were born. With that in mind, let's get to work.

Chapter One

Productivity Is a Priority

*This is the true joy in life, the being used
for a purpose recognized by yourself as
a mighty one; the being thoroughly worn
out before you are thrown on the scrap
heap; the being a force of Nature in-
stead of a feverish selfish little clod of
ailments and grievances complaining
that the world will not devote itself to
making you happy.*
—George Bernard Shaw

Sitting across from my desk was a young
lady who had attended one of my *Life is a Gold
Mine* seminars and wanted to discuss what her
purpose could be. She began, as many people
have over the years, telling me how she had no
idea what her purpose was. "I haven't a clue,"
she said, "and don't know where to look." She
had jotted down some ideas to guide our discussion, but we didn't even get to her notes.

1

I asked her what she liked to do, what her passion was. As is typical for people yet unable to define their purpose, she downplayed and dismissed as insignificant a key interest in her life: she liked to read. "How many books do you read a month?" I asked. She declined to respond, saying that when she told people, they tended to classify her as "strange." But when I encouraged her, she told me, "At least ten."

Ten books a month! And she had been doing this for almost 30 years! When I asked her why she read so much, she responded, "Because I get excited when I learn something new from everything I've read." Although having said that, it was hard—almost impossible—for her to see anything special about this *very special* inclination. As the title of this chapter states, she was being *productive,* not even realizing what she was doing.

Since she was a committed Christian, I then asked about her favorite Bible verses. She told me that she had two. The first was 2 Timothy 1:7, *"For God has not given us the spirit of fear; but of power, and of love, and of a* sound mind*"* (KJV, emphasis added). Her second verse was from Jeremiah 33:3, *"Call to me and I will answer you and tell you great and wonderful things* you do not know*"* (emphasis added).

Here was a woman who had read more than 3,000 books in her lifetime, whom God had promised to give a "sound mind" and that she would learn "wonderful things" she didn't know. Yet she couldn't see that was what she was born to do, because it came naturally to her. It couldn't be the will of God, because it didn't seem spiritual enough, or hard enough, or biblical. Yet this woman was born to learn, and she left my office with a new perspective and a lot to think about. One week later, she found a new job as a research assistant—something that was directly related to her purpose. By the way, she got a $10,000 raise when she started!

She is also investigating how she can share her love for reading and learning with others. Perhaps this search will lead her to a library job or a teaching position. I've found that the critical piece in the purpose puzzle is to find your purpose and then to declare it. Speak it clearly to everyone and anyone. Once that articulation begins to take place, the specific application for that purpose seems to fall into place, taking care of itself.

The power of purpose focuses your life and allows you to find the fulfillment and productivity that you've always wanted. We feel most

3

fulfilled when we are responding to the dreams
God has placed in our hearts and are produc-
tively fulfilling that calling. Don't think for one
minute that God isn't interested in productivity:
He is, and He knows we are happiest when we
are using our talents to the best of our ability.

When God first created Adam and Eve, He
gave them some instructions. *"God blessed them
and said to them, 'Be fruitful and increase in
number; fill the earth and subdue it'"* (Genesis
1:28). The Scriptures also relate that *"the Lord
took the man and put him in the Garden of Eden
to work it and take care of it"* (Genesis 2:15).
God didn't create Adam and Eve—and conse-
quently all of mankind—just to be here on earth
to muddle through life somehow. He put you and
me here to do something specific to serve Him.

Peter, one of Jesus' original disciples and
apostles, wrote the following interesting passage
in his second epistle—one that I pay particular
attention to in my *Life is a Gold Mine* seminar:

> *For this very reason, make every effort to
> add to your faith goodness; and to good-
> ness, knowledge; and to knowledge, self-
> control; and to self-control, perseverance;
> and to perseverance, godliness; and to
> godliness, brotherly kindness; and to*

4

brotherly kindness, love. For if you pos-
sess these qualities in increasing measure,
they will keep you from being ineffective
or unproductive *in your knowledge of our*
Lord Jesus Christ (2 Peter 1:5-8, emphasis
added).

This man, Peter, is an interesting study in
purpose. He was a fisherman working in his
family business when Jesus first met him.
Jesus promised that he would be a "fisher of
men." From that time on, this simple busi-
nessman took on new meaning and purpose
for his life. Eventually, he became the
spokesman and leader for a movement that
would spread throughout the Roman world.
Today, we still study his words and life. He
was not a scholar, nor was he a religious
leader. He was a man who found his purpose; and here I am, 2,000 years later,
quoting from a letter that he wrote.

Notice the emphasis on holiness and right
behavior in those verses, which is where most of
the Church has focused its attention over the
years. But also notice that Peter emphasized
more than holiness. He wrote that you and I
should *increase* in our holiness, or else we may
be found ineffective and unproductive. Let's take

a look at those two words as they appeared in the original Greek that Peter used when he wrote.

The word *ineffective* comes from the Greek word *argos* and is translated "barren" in the more traditional King James version. My research showed that its other meanings included "lazy" and "shunning the labor that one ought to perform." There's a labor that you and I are assigned that is related to our purpose. Finding your purpose releases you to fulfill your labor; it causes you to do things on purpose. And focused labor is not just busywork: focused labor leads to productivity.

There are many people—especially believing Christians—who are content with doctrinal correctness, but stop with that assurance, as if that were all that was needed for them to be in the center of God's will for their lives. They're waiting for God to drop some purpose for them out of the sky that won't require them to work more than the bare minimum required of them. I've known some that have retreated into their families, using the excuse that they can't be at their maximum productivity until their children grow up, their finances improve, or until the system (whether it be political, economic or educational) allows them greater access to power or opportunity. We need to see that there is much we can do right now, using the talents God has given us to their utmost potential.

Many non-Christians in the world follow all kinds of life philosophies that are designed to bring peace and harmony. These are legitimate goals, but what good are they as an end unto themselves? Have those same people founded schools or hospitals? Have they produced movements that have alleviated any world problems? Too often, they are following selfish, self-centered exercises, giving lip service to serving mankind, but in reality focusing primarily on their own individual needs.

It's inconceivable to me that any Christian, who puts his or her faith in the fact that God can raise the dead, can't do exceptional things in this lifetime. But many are content to believe the right thing without ever applying the power of that belief to everyday life. It's not enough to *believe* the right things: we must also *do* the right things. Ours is a faith that works.

Many are also content to lead purposeless lives, feeling that this somehow glorifies the God of creation. This, too, is selfishness and doesn't demonstrate any distinction between a Christian and a non-Christian.

Then there are others who are happy just to

keep busy, without asking whether their busy-
ness is leading to any productive outcome.
Charles Handy wrote in *The Age of Unreason,*

> It is not the devil who finds work for idle
> hands to do, it is our own human in-
> stincts which make us want to contribute
> to our world, to be useful, and to matter
> in some way to other people; to have a
> reason to get up in the morning. To ig-
> nore this instinct to make a difference is
> to ignore one of the basic drives that God
> has given man, a drive to define who he
> is and what God expects him to do.

The Centers for Disease Control and Preven-
tion report that more people die at 9:00 on
Monday morning than at any other time of day
and on any other day of the week. Why? Perhaps
these busy people find no meaning to their work.
They've divorced their existence from any meaningful philosophy of life that allows them to feel
like they're making a difference. Perhaps they
just can't face another meaningless week of
drudgery.

The loss from unproductive lives isn't just in
people dying (and some are "dead" even when
they're alive) before their time. According to

Laurence Boldt, there are greater losses than this:

> Failing to find the work you love has costs, not only to your self-esteem, relationships, health, and creativity, but to your world. As a human community, we all lose when people's creative abilities do not find expression in constructive, purposeful action. We lose in terms of needless human suffering and untapped human potential. Around the globe, useless, even degrading work steals the spirit and saps the joy from the lives of millions, while much necessary work goes undone. Giving your gifts benefits the world, not only through the direct contributions you make and the joy you radiate, but through the living example you provide others of what is possible for them. *Determine to play your part in creating the kind of world you want to live in.*

Now, let's get back to the Bible, Peter, and the second word that I referred to earlier—unproductive. The word *unproductive* comes from the Greek word *akarpos* and is rendered "unfruitful" in the King James Version. It literally means "not yielding the fruit that one ought to yield." The fruit that we are to bear is more than internal: it's also external. It's more than being a nice person. Your "niceness" or kindness should translate into effective labor. It should relate to work that's connected to your purpose in life. Jesus said, *"You did not choose me, but I chose you and appointed you to go and bear fruit, fruit that will remain"* (John 15:16).

Now let's look at some examples of what I would call "fruit." For instance, in his lifetime, Charles Wesley wrote almost 9,000 hymns. Charles' brother, John, preached 40,000 sermons in his lifetime and traveled 250,000 miles on horseback—the equivalent of 10 circuits of the globe along the equator. Charles Haddon Spurgeon, the great British 19th-century preacher, preached to 10 million in his lifetime!

But let's look outside the realm of church or missions work. Cyrus McCormick, 19th-century inventor and business innovator, not only invented the reaper, but also created such "modern" business techniques as the written money-back guarantee, a guaranteed sale price to buyers, interest-free financing to farmers who desperately needed the equipment, and service and repairs for the machines he sold.

George Washington Carver, the African-American 19th-century scientist, discovered more than 300 uses for the peanut and more than 100 uses for the sweet potato, thus providing much-needed markets for crops unique to the southern area of the United States.

How productive are you? What are you doing *on purpose*? Is your increasing knowledge of God leading to effectiveness and productivity? Or are you content to sit back, smugly satisfied that your life philosophy and beliefs are all that is required of you? Before you go on, reflect on these questions. Write down where your thoughts lead you. In the next chapter, I want to encourage you to get more specific about your purpose, for without that, you can't hope to fulfill God's desire (or your own) for productivity and meaning.

What is your greatest area of *productivity?* Is it cooking? One woman told me that she sensed "the presence of God" every time she opened her oven door and felt the heat caress her face. Is it baking? I talked with a woman in Montana who was known as the "cookie lady." People told me that she "constantly" made cookies, put a few of them in plastic bags, attached a little piece of paper with a Bible verse on it, and went through their small town distributing them to those she met. We may find that our own purpose is cooking or baking *within us,* just waiting to come out of the oven so others can enjoy it.

What is your greatest area of *effectiveness*? Is it people in need? Or little people? A recent issue of *Southern Living* magazine talked about a man named Doyle Cagle, who some would say is "just" a school bus driver. But this bus driver gives $3 out of his own pocket to the children on his bus who make the honor roll. If a child forgets his backpack, Mr. Cagle goes back to get it and deliver it to the child at school. He belongs to the PTA for all three schools to which he delivers children. One parent said, "Every child thinks Mr. Cagle likes him best. He is what God wants us to be." Who does God want *you* to be?

Chapter Two

Productivity Requires Purpose

One purpose of life is to discover who we are. Finding out who we are, though, is not as easy as it would seem. We are so much a part of the group that we have to listen very closely to discover our inner self . . . what our uniqueness is. It is when we finally hear the truth of ourselves that we discover our own creativity. This process of self-discovery is as important as the possible products of that discovery.

—Joyce Wycoff

What Would You Write?

When I begin an all-day seminar to help people better define their purpose, I often ask the participants to make an attempt to define their purpose. But what about you, the reader? What is your purpose in life? Please write it down in the space provided.

_____

_____

_____

When asked the same question, some will stare at me, not knowing what to write, since no one has ever asked them to put their purpose on paper. Others will make an attempt, writing simply, "to do the will of God," "to worship the Lord," "to glorify God," "to help people" or "to serve mankind." These answers aren't really wrong: they simply lack the focus and definition needed to help you know what it is that constitutes "doing God's will" or "worshiping Him." I've found these words of Jesus helpful:

> *Father, the time has come. Glorify your Son, that your Son may glorify you. For you have granted him authority over all people that he might give eternal life to all those you have given him. Now this is eternal life: that they may know you, the only true God, and Jesus Christ, whom*

you have sent. I have brought you glory on earth by completing the work you gave me to do (John 17:1-4, emphasis added).

Jesus brought "glory to God" by completing the work God gave Him to do. You'll do the same as you find your purpose and make every effort to fulfill it. This isn't always easy, and many people shy away from the process, intuitively sensing that it can be a tough and painful journey of self-analysis and soul-searching. But Richard Bolles, who has authored the annually updated best-seller, *What Color is Your Parachute?*, writes these words that should encourage you in this search process:

But having to wait for the voice of God to reveal what our Mission is, is not the truest picture of our situation. St. Paul, in Romans, speaks of a law "written in our members"—and this phrase has a telling application to the question of *how* God reveals to each of us our unique Mission in life. Read again the definition of our third Mission (above) and you will see: the clear implication of the definition is that God has *already* revealed His will to us concerning our vocation and Mission, by causing it to be *"written in our members."* We are to begin deciphering our unique Mission by studying our talents and skills, and more particularly which ones (or one) we most rejoice to use.

God actually has written His will twice in our members: first in the talents which He lodged there, and secondly in His guidance of our heart, as to which talent gives us the greatest pleasure from its exercise *(it is usually the one which, when we use it, causes us to lose all sense of time).*

Even as the anthropologist can examine ancient inscriptions, and divine from them the daily life of a long lost people, so we by examining *our talents* and *our heart* can more often than we dream divine the Will of the Living God. For true it is, our Mission is not something He *will* reveal; it is something He *has already* revealed. It is not to be found written in the sky; it is to be found written in our members.

Recognizing what's already "written in your members" (Romans 7:23) will lead you to happiness and true effectiveness, which is defined by *Vine's Dictionary of Old and New Testament Words* as "being full of power to achieve results." You don't want to play business, school or church. You should want to get results, and you'll get those results most often when you are functioning in your purpose.

My purpose is to bring *order out of chaos.* (I explain in detail on the audio tape previously mentioned, how I came to that conclusion.) I continue to do that on a daily basis; and when I do, I feel most fulfilled. In keeping with my pattern, I still haven't looked for a job in my entire adult life. My jobs, including my current positions, have just "come" to me. I also have the privilege of traveling and helping others find their purpose, not because I'm a great teacher, but because helping you find your purpose is part of my purpose of bringing order out of chaos.

This purpose is consistent with who I am. I like to think of myself as organized, focused, disciplined, and task-oriented. I'm also practical: I prefer to look at the bottom line. The words "order out of chaos" are simply a concise way of describing the gift package and life philosophy that has always been with me.

The power of purpose is such that God wants you to fulfill it more than you do. He created you with a purpose in mind—one that will benefit you and everyone that comes into contact with you. If you'll identify, verbalize, and take steps to strengthen your purpose, God will bring more than enough opportunities for you to express it. In fact, you've probably already been expressing it without even realizing it.

As you can tell, I enjoy reading and studying the Bible. It's a relevant book for modern man, even though some of it is 4,000 years old! Let me give you some other biblical and first-hand examples of people who found that they were doing things "on purpose." Perhaps they will "stir your pot" or "prime your pump" so that you can identify your own purpose.

Biblical Examples

I think that, with a little work, you can identify the life's purpose of anyone in the Bible. I offer the following examples as proof:

- Jesus—to seek and save the lost (Luke 19:10)
- Adam—be fruitful, multiply, fill the earth and subdue it (Genesis 1:28)
- Eve—to be a helper suitable to Adam (Genesis 2:18)
- Abraham—to be a great nation (Genesis 12:2)

- Joseph—to rule over his father's sons (Genesis 37:8)
- Joshua—to lead the people into the land (Joshua 1:6)
- David—to be king over Israel (1 Samuel 16:12-13)
- Isaiah—to "go and tell this people" (Isaiah 9:6)
- Jeremiah—to be a prophet to the nations (Jeremiah 1:5)
- Daniel—to be a source of wisdom, knowledge and discernment (Daniel 2:21)
- John the Baptist—to prepare the way of the Lord (Matthew 3:3)
- Mary, Jesus' mother—to believe all that the Lord spoke to her (Luke 1:45)
- Andrew and Peter—to be fishers of men (Matthew 4:19)

Do you see how easy it is to identify purpose, once you know what to look for? Why not do some research of your own? See if you can identify and write out the purpose of the people listed by looking up the reference(s) provided.

Moses_____
_____ (Acts 7:25; Exodus 2:14).

Deborah_____
_____ (Judges 4:4-5,15).

Solomon_____
_____ (1 Kings 1:13, 4:29-34).

Esther_____
_____ (Esther 4:14)

Nehemiah_____
_____ (Nehemiah 2:1-20)

Joseph_____
_____(Matthew 1:20-25; John 6:42).

The Apostle Peter_____
_____ (Matthew 4:18, 16:18-19; Galatians 2:7-8).

The Apostle Paul_____
_____ (Acts 26:9-21).

I know what you're thinking: "What about me? Those were biblical people and it was somehow easier for them than it is for me." For some more examples of practical purpose statements from modern day men and women, we return to *What Color is Your Parachute?*

Your unique and individual mission will most likely turn out to be a mission of love, acted out in one or all of three arenas: either in the kingdom of the mind, whose goal is to bring more truth into the world; or in the kingdom of the heart, whose goal is to bring more beauty into the world; or in the kingdom of the will, whose goal is to bring more perfection into the world, through service. Here are some examples:

• "My mission is, out of the rich reservoir of love which God seems to have given me, to nurture and show love to others—most particularly to those who are suffering from incurable diseases."

• "My mission is to draw maps for people to show them how to get to God."

• "My mission is to create the purest foods I can, to help people's bodies not get in the way of their spiritual growth."

• "My mission is the make the finest harps I can so that people can hear the voice of God in the wind."

• "My mission is to make people laugh, so that the travail of this earthly life doesn't seem quite so hard to them."

• "My mission is to help people know the truth, in love, about what is happening out in the world, so that there will be more honesty in the world."

• "My mission is to weep with those who weep, so that in my arms they may feel themselves in the arms of that Eternal Love which sent me and which created them."

• "My mission is to create beautiful gardens, so that in the lilies of the field people may behold the Beauty of God and be reminded of the Beauty of Holiness" (pp.228-9).

These statements are beautiful expressions of the individuality given to each person by his or her Creator. In the examples above, each person had a clear, concise statement that summarized his or her existence. They were specific enough to give direction, but general enough to give room for creative expression. You need that same clarity if you want the best chance to be effective and productive.

I also like the arenas that Bolles creates to categorize life purpose or mission. They are: 1) *the kingdom of the mind*—to bring truth into the world; 2) *the kingdom of the heart*—to bring more beauty into the world; and 3) *the kingdom of the will*—to bring more perfection into the world, through service.

In which of these three arenas do you tend to function? As you move toward making a clear statement, it's important that you place yourself in one of those three categories. You personally are not exclusively restricted to one category, but your mission will emphasize one more directly than the others. In the next chapter, we'll continue the process of finding a statement that describes what's already "written in your members." An anonymous author from the book *Theologia Germanica,* written in the 14th century, has the following encouraging words on the value of finding our own purpose:

> Therefore, although it be good and profitable that we should ask, and learn and know what good and holy men have wrought and suffered, and how God hath dealt with them, and what he hath wrought in and through them, yet *it were a thousand times better that we should in ourselves learn and perceive and understand, who we are, how and what our own life is, what God is and what he is doing in us, what he will have from us, and to what ends he will or will not make use of us.* For, of a truth, thoroughly to know oneself, is above all art, for it is the highest art. If thou knowest thyself well, thou art better and, more praiseworthy before God, than if thou didst not know thyself, but didst understand the course of the heavens and of all the planets and stars, also the virtue of all herbs, and the structure and dispositions of all mankind, also the nature of all beasts,

and, in such matters, hadst all the skill of all who are in heaven and on earth. For it is said, there came a voice from heaven, saying, "Man, know thyself."

Chapter Three

Purpose Is Personal and Progressive

To the extent that your work takes into account the needs of the world, it will be meaningful to the extent that through it you express your unique talents, it will be joyful.
—Laurence G. Boldt, *How to Find the Work You Love*

I was in Wichita, Kansas conducting another all-day purpose seminar. As was my custom, I had sent the participants off to lunch with a simple assignment: to ask those with whom they had come (who were attending a seminar other than mine) to describe how they saw them. I found that this often helped my "students" see their purpose more clearly.

On this particular day, I called on one woman to give me her report, and she proceeded

25

to share with me the following story: "Well, when I asked people what they thought my purpose was, they began to describe me using words like 'joy,' 'rejoicing,' and 'happiness.' My favorite verse from the Bible is Nehemiah 8:10, which states, *'The joy of the Lord is my* [your] *strength.'* But joy couldn't be my purpose, could it?"

The interesting thing wasn't just what she told me, but *how* she told it to me. The whole time she was talking before the class, she had this huge smile frozen across her face. In fact, her whole body seemed to smile. I asked her what she did in her church, and she told me that she was the song leader. When I asked her what feedback she got from her leading, she replied, "People always tell me they love to watch me because they feel so uplifted and happy when I sing."

I then said to her jokingly, "I'll bet you hear bad news, and it takes you a week to figure out that it's bad." She immediately responded that people had accused her of ignoring reality or having her head in the clouds. But she said, "I figure, why let stuff like that get you down."

Here was a woman whose purpose it was to bring God's joy into any situation in which she found herself. God had given her some part of His own character, so that when people touched her joy, they would actually be coming into contact with an aspect of God Himself. In a world filled with sadness and grief, that woman's purpose of joy was certain to be in great demand. She left the seminar with a whole new sense of self-awareness and direction.

Your purpose is *personal.* The Lord can take a simple phrase, mentioned by someone else or in the Bible, and quicken it to you, so that it brings you much-needed definition and understanding. Others can hear that word or phrase and it will not mean anything to them; but for you that word becomes personal, defining why you were born.

The purpose of the woman mentioned above was to bring joy, and her joy was increased with the recognition of her purpose. I have found joy to be the common denominator in the lives of people who know their purpose. In the movie, "Chariots of Fire," Eric Liddell, a missionary statesman, truly rejoiced in his God-given purpose at the time—running. He gave a classic response to his sister when he said, "But God made me fast, and when I run, I feel His pleasure." If you can find what gives you pleasure when you do it, then you are close to defining your own purpose. It's as simple as that.

Only you can identify this personal joy—the exhilaration that you feel when you are doing something that gives you a sense of meaning and fulfillment. Immanuel Kant, the famous philosopher, said, "Joy is an indication of purpose." I'm not saying that purpose is easy or without its difficult work. In fact, joy is the fuel that can keep you going through the tough assignments that often come when you function in your purpose.

John Piper, in his book *Desiring God: Meditations of a Christian Hedonist,* wrote that once you see that world of purpose, it will become more clear to you over time just how significant it is, and how you can use it to serve God and be effective. That's why I say that it's *progressive.* Look at what Paul wrote about the progressive nature and understanding of his purpose:

> *I did not receive it* [the Gospel to the Gentiles] *from any man, nor was I taught it; rather, I received it by revelation from Jesus Christ. . . .But when God, who set me apart from birth and called me by his grace, was pleased to reveal his Son in me so that I might preach him among the Gentiles, I did*

not consult any man, nor did I go up to Jerusalem to see those who were apostles before I was, . . .Then after three years, I went up to Jerusalem to get acquainted with Peter and stayed with him fifteen days. . . .Fourteen years later I went up again to Jerusalem, this time with Barnabas . . . and set before them the gospel that I preach among the Gentiles. . . .They saw that I had been entrusted with the task of preaching the gospel to the Gentiles, just as Peter had been to the Jews (Galatians 1:12,15-16,18, 2:1-2,7).

Even though Paul had a dramatic encounter where his purpose was revealed to him (see Acts 26:9-19), he still had a progressive understanding of what he was to do and how he was to do it. Even though he had companions on that road who saw the light and knew that something had happened, only Saul heard the voice and knew what it meant. He had a *personal* encounter.

As I've worked with people to help them find their purpose, I've seen some powerful encounters as individuals have come to know their personal purpose. I've watched them progress as they've seen just what the Lord had in mind when He assigned them their purpose. Let me give you a few examples.

Jim Newsom

My friend, Jim, formed a church in Orlando, Florida, and then invited me to come and pastor there for a season. At the same time, Jim also invited me to sit on the board of his prison ministry. I accepted that position and, for the next four years, Jim and I traveled to jails and prisons conducting seminars and workshops.

While ministering with Jim, I noticed how he would find the best in every situation and every person. I thought Jim was just trying to make the best of what I saw as bad situations, but this pattern continued. Then one day, while seeking the Lord for his purpose, Jim came into my office and announced he had found his purpose. He read me Jeremiah 15:19 from the New American Standard Version: *"If you'll extract the precious from the worthless, you'll be my spokesman."*

I saw that Jim wasn't just trying to find the

best in people and circumstances: He was doing what he was born to do. And today, he has progressively grown in that purpose to the point that he is in demand nationally as a speaker and retreat leader. The fact that Jim had served eight years of a 30-year sentence for second-degree murder only adds credence to the power behind personal purpose. If his sin didn't disqualify him, then yours won't keep you from fulfilling your purpose. If God did it for him, He can do it for you!

Ron Kenoly

When I worked for Worship International, I had the privilege of working, ministering, and traveling with many great musical ministers. One of my favorites was Ron Kenoly. Ron today travels the world, leading large crowds in worship and praise. When I asked Ron what his purpose was, he responded, "To sing." Now, normally I would see that description as simplistic and try to bring something more defined out of the individual responding; but with Ron, there was no need—he truly was born to sing.

Ron told me of how he had not been involved in church work for many years, and during that time, sang in night clubs. When his wife and mother prayed him back to the Lord, he began to sing for the Lord wherever he could find an opening. Oftentimes, he didn't even receive enough in return to cover his expenses. But he kept singing.

Then, Ron told me of a two-and-a-half hour concert he did one night in a church. On that particular night, there was only one person present—and it was the Lord. Ron walked out of that church and told the Lord that he was going to keep singing, if for no one else but for Him. And Ron's purpose kept urging him on and driving him to fulfill what he was born to do.

Ron became Music Minister at Jubilee Christian Fellowship in San Jose, California, and gave himself to the work of that ministry. He wrote the now popular song, "Jesus Is Alive," as part of an Easter musical for his church. He was then "discovered" by the executives at Integrity Music, and the rest is history. His worship recordings have sold more copies than any other musical worship projects in history.

Why has Ron been so successful? At least part of his success can be attributed to his clear, personal understanding of what he was born to do, and his coming to progressively understand that purpose and how it was to be achieved. Truly this man was born to sing, and when he does, he feels God's pleasure flow through him and those to whom he is singing.

Brother Art

In 1995, I conducted a purpose seminar in Morgantown, West Virginia, at the invitation of my good friend and fellow minister, Ron Wood. It was open to the public, and Brother Art, an 82 year old man, came to the seminar. He openly stated that he was coming to make some sense of his life, which, for him at least, made no sense. As the day went on, Art and all present found that purpose is indeed personal and progressive.

Art asked me during the day to help him define his purpose. When I asked him what he thought his purpose was, he responded, "to help people." I again felt this was a little vague and began to ask him some questions. But his answers only served to confirm what he felt and to help bring him much-needed understanding that he had been on target most of his life.

Art told me that he was a retired engineer. All his life he had sat at his drafting table or work cubicle, and all his life people had felt free to come to him for help. He shared with the seminar class how he had gone out of his way to help people, doing things for them that were beyond the normal call of Christian duty. Art also shared that he had a 17-page prayer list consisting of the names of people he had met over the years, for whom he had prayed daily! He closed out our discussion by telling us how he was currently working on raising $250,000 for a scholarship fund for disadvantaged students in West Virginia.

Truly this man was born "to help people." At the end of the day, he came up to me with tears in his eyes and thanked me. He told me, "All my life I've felt like I've missed the mark and didn't use my life as it could or should have been used. Today, I saw that wasn't true."

How about you? Are you overlooking the obvious? Do you have a simple, yet profound and personal phrase or statement that summarizes your life and existence? Is that statement something that sounds good but has no proof in practical experience, or have you seen it progressively unfold in your life? Can others see it and "bear witness" to its truth? Every purpose demands proof, and you must find that place of productivity that only comes from knowing and doing (or being) your purpose.

Chapter Four

Purpose Demands Proof

You see that a person is justified by what he does and not by faith alone (James 2:24).

If you haven't yet noticed it, each chapter so far has contained words that begin with the letter "P." We have seen that *p*roductivity is a *p*riority, that *p*roductivity requires that you function in your *p*urpose, and that *p*urpose is *p*ersonal and *p*rogressive. The next few chapters continue this same trend. I'm not sure why I did this, except that it was fun and a challenge. Remember, I like to bring order out of chaos. This may not seem like a big thing to you, but it is to me and my unusual sense of order! In this chapter, we'll discuss the fact that *p*urpose demands *p*roof.

Biblical Evidence

My quest to understand my purpose began

one day in my Mobile Business Service office when I was meditating on a verse from the Bible. Genesis 1:2 states, *"Now the earth was formless and empty, darkness was over the surface of the deep, and the Spirit of God was hovering over the waters."* It was my research of that verse that led me to identify the phrase "order out of chaos" as my life's purpose.

This phrase accurately describes my life as I've understood it and as others have commented on it. I've always been chosen to organize things, and people have commented on how structured I am and how organized I can be. I feel my greatest sense of peace and joy when I've organized a large conference or tour, or when I've tackled a tough problem and found the solution. There's physical proof in my life that bringing order out of chaos is my life's purpose.

My point is that my first clue came from the Bible. I stated in the Introduction that my premise for all this is that your Creator holds the keys that unlock your purpose. The focal point for God's revelation to man is the Bible, so I expect that living Book to help bring definition to God's creatures. As Joseph Garlington, my pastor, is fond of saying, "The Bible is the oldest book written whose author is still alive!" This very-much-alive Author can and does orchestrate this process, and His help is our only hope to find and fulfill our purpose to the fullest.

Jesus' purpose is found in the story of a tax collector named Zacchaeus, found in Luke 19. As Jesus came into Jericho with His entourage, He called that little man down from his vantage point up in the sycamore tree. The entire group then went to Zacchaeus' home for a meal, and the host chose that event to announce some shocking news:

> *Look, Lord! Here and now I give half of my possessions to the poor, and if I have cheated anybody out of anything, I will pay back four times the amount* (Luke 19:8).

Jesus replied,

> *Today salvation has come to this house, because this man, too, is a son of Abraham. For the Son of Man came to seek and to save what was lost* (Luke 19:9).

That phrase represents Jesus' life purpose as

well as anything He ever said. But more on that practical (another word that begins with "P") aspect later.

Even Jesus had biblical "evidence" for His purpose. To see that, we need only look earlier in Luke's Gospel.

He [Jesus]*went to Nazareth, where he had been brought up, and on the Sabbath day he went into the synagogue as was his custom. And he stood up to read. The scroll of the prophet Isaiah was handed to him. Unrolling it, he found the place where it is written: The Spirit of the Lord is on me, Because he has anointed me To preach good news to the poor. He has sent me to proclaim freedom For the prisoners And recovery of sight for the blind, To release the oppressed, To proclaim the year of the Lord's favor.' Then he rolled up the scroll, gave it back to the attendant and sat down. The eyes of everyone in the synagogue were fastened upon him, and he began by saying to them, "Today this scripture is fulfilled in your hearing"* (Luke 4:14-21).

This passage that Jesus read is from what

we identify today to be Isaiah 61:1-2. How beautifully and accurately those verses describe what we know of Jesus' earthly ministry, which was an expression of His purpose "to seek and save what was lost." Not only was Jesus clear on what He was to do, He was clear on the biblical description and authorization for what He was doing. The biblical context is an important piece of the purpose puzzle for you and me.

Jesus was not alone in knowing this biblical perspective for His purpose. When the Pharisees pressed John the Baptist—Jesus' cousin and a prophet—for an answer to the question, "Who are you?" he responded by saying, "*I am the voice of one calling in the desert, 'Make straight the way of the Lord'*" (John 1:23). He was referring to Isaiah 40:3. Somewhere, somehow, the Lord had made this verse a personal "motto" for this great prophet.

When the Apostles Paul and Barnabas were on their first missions journey, they were preaching in a synagogue in a city called Pisidian Antioch and were challenged by unbelieving and jealous Jews.

Then Paul and Barnabas answered them boldly: "We had to speak the word of

God to you first. Since you reject it and do not consider yourselves worthy of eternal life, we now turn to the Gentiles. For this is what the Lord has commanded us: 'I have made you a light for the Gentiles, That you may bring salvation to the ends of the earth.'" When the Gentiles heard this, they were glad and honored the word of the Lord; and all who were appointed for eternal life believed (Acts 13:46-48).

Paul and Barnabas were quoting Isaiah 49:6. Obviously, they had seen the Old Testament truth that the Gospel was to be taken to the Gentiles. While others read those verses and were unaffected, Paul and Barnabas saw those particular verses and "knew" them to be more than just theological truth. Those verses were the very basis for their existence and evidence for their purpose.

What's your defining verse, passage, chapter or book from the Bible? Very often people will refer to something as a favorite verse or passage, but it may be more. Could it hold a clue to your purpose? I challenge you to find your life's verse and identify it, so that it can fit alongside your purpose statement.

Practical Evidence

I've met some who have a "verse," but not much practical evidence to go with it. It isn't enough to have a phrase to describe your purpose if you never accomplish anything that proves the truth of that phrase. As someone once said, "Wishing it so doesn't make it so!" I can point to a number of "proofs" that my purpose is to bring order out of chaos—not off in some laboratory, but in real life situations.

Jesus had practical evidence to go with His verses and purpose statement. Jesus did seek the lost, and He gathered quite a crowd of prostitutes, tax collectors, broken people and other "sinners" around Him wherever He went. And often, when He wasn't seeking the lost, the lost were seeking Him.

Consider the story in John 4 of the woman at Jacob's well. Jesus was resting at the well while His disciples went to get food. A woman who had been married five times and was then living with a man just "happened" to come to the well for water. Jesus engaged her in conversation and soon revealed her life's secrets. This conversation caused the woman to go back to her home village and bring others to hear this man who had lovingly confronted her empty life.

When one lives out his or her purpose, that purpose will lead to proof, because purpose is *active.* It's always seeking to do and accomplish in order to touch a needy world and its inhabitants. What type or group of people has consistently sought you out for help during your lifetime? What business opportunities constantly find you, even when you're not looking for them? What effect have you brought on a regular basis to your work, family, ministry or coincidental meetings with people? Answers to those questions can lead to understanding your purpose. There's always evidence to go with a purpose, even when you weren't able to define it!

John the Baptist was to "make straight the way of the Lord." So what did he do? He went into the desert where no one else lived, had a wardrobe that no one else shared, ate food that no one else ate, and preached a message that no one else liked. You might say he was a bit eccentric.

Even though he lived in the desert, the entire nation turned out to see and hear him—even those who didn't respond to or appreciate his message. And many did prepare their hearts for the messenger who was to succeed John. God was with him when he made straight the way of the Lord. There was evidence to validate his purpose.

Then there was the Apostle Paul: he took a message of the covenant that had been the exclusive property of the Jews and went to the Gentiles. He came unannounced and had to work with idolaters and those who had no experience with the Old Testament or heritage like Paul did. Yet look what happened: everywhere Paul went he left a church made up of believers who were from Jewish and Gentile backgrounds.

Paul proceeded to leave a body of material that would impact the Gentile world for centuries to come. His writings provide the evidence that Paul was born to preach the Gospel to the Gentiles. When he did, God was with him and there was fruit and confirming evidence that he was on the right path.

What evidence is in your life, which is so obvious that you may be overlooking it? Do people compliment you on your hospitality and ability to make people feel at home? Do you then dismiss it by saying, "Yes, my grandmother owned a restaurant, and I used to work there during my summers. . . . But that's not significant. If I could only sing like Amy Grant, then God could really use me."

Do people tell you that you have a way of finding mechanical problems and fixing them, only to have you respond, "Well, my dad had a shop, and we used to work in it together. . . . But that's nothing: if I could only preach like Billy Graham, then God could really use me."

Or do folks tell you that you're easy to talk to and that they feel comfortable sharing their life and even their secrets with you? Do you say in response, "Oh, my mother was a polite person and taught me how to listen to people and act like I'm interested. . . . But if I could only help the poor like Mother Teresa, then God could really use me."

I've got news for you. If you fit into any of the above categories or have a similar category—God's already using you! Don't look for the hard thing, the super-spiritual thing or the thing you think God or others want you to do or be. Look to the *evidence*, both biblical and practical, and ask God to show you who you are. If it's good enough for Him, shouldn't it be good enough for you? If it's important to Him that He created you as you are, shouldn't it be important to you?

Don't let the seeming difficulty of finding your purpose stop you from trying. After all, every servant has one right, and that is to know the will of the Master. If God wants you to do His will, He must show you what it is, or He can't expect you to do it. And we know that He wiil show us if we ask Him. You can define your purpose in clear, concise terms: you just need the right inspiration and motivation.

What Were Your Childhood Dreams?

Very often your childhood daydreams hold clues to your life's purpose. Denis Waitley, well-known author and teacher, affirms this tendency in his book, *Empires of the Mind.* Consider the early fantasies of these famous people:

• His love of woodworking and violin music began in childhood.
   —*Antonio Stradivari*
• As a child in England, he spent hours creating cardboard sets for his puppet shows to entertain his family.
   —*Andrew Lloyd Webber*
• Cut from his basketball team as a youngster, he still dreamed of playing.
   —*Michael Jordan*
• Swimming to gain strength in his two broken arms, the teenager changed dreams from astronaut to aquanaut.
   —*Jacques Cousteau*
• The young boy was fascinated with

anatomical diagrams in the World Book.
>   —*Jonas Salk,* inventor of
>   the polio vaccine

• At twenty-one, she lived in a one-room flat over her father's grocery store and dreamed of public service.
>   —*Margaret Thatcher*

• A high-school term paper was on being a cook and owning a restaurant.
>   —*Dave Thomas,* founder of
>   Wendy's hamburger chain

• This college dropout had ideas about information access.
>   —Bill Gates

What about you? What did you dream about when you were growing up? Can your early years provide any proof or evidence of your purpose? Does your dream hold clues to your purpose? Are you doing today what you dreamed about, or can you begin doing it at this stage of your life?

I can remember my early childhood, rainy day game of "office." I would create messy stacks of papers and then sit down at my toy typewriter and straighten my office. These were early signs of my propensity to bring order out of chaos! In Waitley's book, *The New Dynamics of Goal Setting*, he shares his story:

Can you remember what you really wanted as a child? When I was a young boy I had a recurring fantasy of standing in a beautiful theater like Lincoln Center or Radio City Music Hall in New York. I was wearing a tuxedo, and I was bowing to an appreciative audience after some kind of performance, with my mother, father, sister, brother, and grandparents smiling in the front row. This vision began when I was nine and continued for many years . . . until I found myself, not too long ago, in a tuxedo, speaking to an audience in Carnegie Hall in New York. My parents and family weren't in the front row, as they had been in my fantasy, but everything else about the setting was nearly identical!

Identifying a childhood "fantasy" can help you identify how close you are to fulfilling that supposed fantasy now, and help you see it as part of your purpose. Is there evidence to go with that fantasy that will help you clarify your mission in life?

Chapter Five

Purpose Is Practical

Everybody can be great. Because everybody can serve. You don't have to have a college degree to serve. You don't have to make your subject and verb agree to serve. You don't have to know about Plato and Aristotle. . . Einstein's Theory of Relativity. . . [or] the Second Theory of Thermodynamics in physics to serve. You only need a heart full of grace. A soul generated by love.
—Martin Luther King

I was in Oklahoma City conducting my purpose seminar when a woman approached me after the class. I had mentioned that I was living in Mobile, and she related how she herself was connected to Mobile through an association with the Junior Miss Society as their Oklahoma state director. She asked if I would be willing to come sometime and speak to her colleagues at the Junior Miss organization.

Over the years, I've had many people come forward to ask me a similar question, and seldom has anyone followed up on the inquiry. But this woman in Oklahoma City did, and several months later, I found myself speaking at a retreat attended by every state director and the Junior Miss Board of Directors.

Since you know my purpose, you know why I was there. Without knowing it, the Society was going through some chaos, and I was there to bring order! I shared what I knew to say and found out later that my input had helped turn the organization around. They invited me back to speak at their opening breakfast that year, and I had a chance to talk to 50 of the finest high school senior girls in the United States. And you know I talked to them about purpose!

My purpose has not taken me away from people or real-life situations and problems. Yours won't either. My purpose is practical: it allows me to help people, and some I've been able to help on a deep, spiritual level as God has opened the doors.

Too often, people whom I have talked to about purpose consider purpose as something only for the famous or super-spiritual. Or, they are often content to define purpose in hard-to-understand terms, thinking their definition brings meaning to every day life. Nothing could be further from the truth.

Years ago, I had the privilege of baptizing a Chinese young man who was studying in the United States. This man had decided to become a follower of Jesus, and for him that meant entering the baptismal waters. As he stood waist deep in that pool, he asked for his Chinese Bible and turned to John 3:16. He read in Chinese and translated for us in English. When he did, he put a new twist into a familiar passage when he translated, "For God so loved *people* that He gave. . . ." Now that is not accurate to the original Greek translation, but it is still true. God loves people. He loves them so much that He made you and me. And when He made us, He gave us a purpose—some part of Himself—so that when people touch us, they are touching part of Him! Don't dismiss this thought as weird—it's true!

If you are a good listener, so is God. If you can extract the precious from the worthless, so can God. Your ability to function in your purpose through the power of God is proof of God's love, not just for you, but for the people around you.

I can bring order out of chaos because that is a part of who God is. *"God is not a God of disorder, but of peace"* (1 Corinthians 14:33). When I function in my purpose, I'm expressing one particular aspect of God's love and care to the world around me. And that care demonstrates itself in practical ways, even to some people and organizations that I didn't even know God was interested in. But He is, because God loves people. And as I have often said somewhat jokingly, God is the best administrator I've ever met.

Consider one aspect of this truth from the Old Testament:

> *Then the Lord said to Moses, "See, I have chosen Bezalel son of Uri, the son of Hur, of the tribe of Judah, and I have filled him with the Spirit of God, with skill, ability and knowledge in all kinds of crafts—to make artistic designs for work in gold, silver and bronze, to cut and set stones, to work in wood, and to engage in all kinds of craftsmanship. Moreover, I have appointed Oholiah son of Ahismach, of the tribe of Dan, to help him"* (Exodus 31:1-6).

Notice that Bezalel was "filled with the Spirit of God" not to preach, do church work, sing songs, or write books. He was filled with God's Spirit to work with his hands! He had a practical craft whose source was spiritual. Bezalel could have dismissed this as insignificant or just a talent he had or training that he had received from his father. But God saw his skill from a different perspective.

First and foremost, Bezalel's purpose was to serve God's purpose. But his purpose was practical! He brought beauty out of raw materials. This beauty brought people's attention to God's creation and led people to worship in the tabernacle that God designed but that Bezalel helped build. God is not removed from the everyday affairs of men and women. He has created you and wants you to be His agent here as you function in your purpose. And God may want you to bring beauty into the lives of others through music, dance, or some other creative expression.

Notice also that Bezalel had a helper whose name was Oholiab. Oholiab wasn't just hired help; he wasn't somebody's flunkey. He was appointed by God to assist the "main man." His "help" wasn't just an occupation, it was his life's purpose. I have to believe that God was with him and showed him how to be a good helper, because God comes along side us and helps you and me when we function in our purpose. Oholiab was simply expressing some aspect of God's personality to the world around him; and he was serving God working in the metal shop.

When Adam was created, God told him to *"Be fruitful and increase in number; fill the earth and subdue it"* (Genesis 1:28). That was utterly practical! Adam was to work at having a family and at subduing the earth. His purpose was to *"rule over the fish of the sea and the birds of the air and over every living creature that moves on the ground"* (Genesis 1:29). That did not involve church work.

Now you may think that I am against church work. And sometimes I am—when it becomes, in someone's mind, the only way that a person can please God or be used by Him. If you were born to fulfill your purpose in church work, then do it with all the strength that God provides. If you weren't, then stop trying to be what you are not. Maybe you were born for business, art, movies or computers. Maybe God wants to send you to Babylon like He sent Daniel to express your purpose (and God's love) for some foreign culture and people.

If you try to be something that God never intended you to be, then you are trying to improve on what God has made you. And that's not right. If you are good enough for God, why would you try to go against the counsel of His will and be something you think would honor Him? Be yourself and allow God to invest you in whatever way He chooses, according to the purpose He has given you. And look for ways to be practical, and that means looking for ways to help people. Laurie Jones, in her best-selling book, *The Path,* writes,

> Every mission implies that someone will be helped. A nation will be freed, a bird will be returned to its nest again, a child will have a new image of what parental love can be. Whom is it that you were sent here to help?

> The more specific you can be, the more focused and powerful will be your energy. Jesus said, *"I came to help the lost sheep of Israel"* and was reluctant to turn his attention to the Gentiles, knowing that someone would follow in his footsteps to undertake that specific task—namely, Peter. Because he was clear on his "for whom" he stayed

within a 30-mile radius of his home, teaching, healing, and preaching primarily to "the lost sheep of Israel." His specific "for whom" enabled him to keep his focus.

Let's return to Laurence Boldt and his book, *How to Find the Work You Love.* This is what he writes concerning the issue of your purpose and how it relates to the world around you.

Consider as an example of traditional vocational theory a simple formula given by the Greek philosopher, Aristotle. He said, "Where your talents and the needs of the world cross, there lies your vocation." This simple statement tells you everything you need to know to find the work you love. . . . to suggest that when making vocational choices, we ought to look for an intersection between our individual talents and the needs of the world implies that human happiness springs from individual creative expression and meaningful participation in the life of society.

Within Aristotle's simple formula, there lies a profound understanding of human nature. In effect, he is saying that because we are social beings, we ought to look to, become aware of, and identify the needs of the world; and because we are individuals, we ought to look to, become aware of, and identify our own unique talents. Furthermore, he is suggesting that these two elements of our nature not only can but in fact ought to be in harmony. As social beings, our interest in the needs of the world is not a matter of doing good for others out of a sense of largess. It's a matter of being true to ourselves.

Remember, God loves the world and people. He created you to be a gift to the world (and people) as you express your individual purpose in some practical way. If you are good enough for God, don't try to imitate someone else who is functioning successfully in their purpose and think that you are pleasing God. You're not! Be yourself and go with the flow. In the end, you'll be content as you feel God's pleasure helping you be who He made you to be.

My Sister-in-Law

My wife's sister, Diana, hasn't worked in decades. Let me explain. She had a good job with the National Chamber of Commerce, but quit to travel the world. She came home and worked out of her Washington, D.C. condominium as a writer. Then, she held a position as editor for a Christian magazine, but left that to move to Orlando, Florida. Today, she sits at home; well, while she sits, she writes. And her writing provides her means of support.

Diana has found her purpose, and it is practical. It allows her to take her talents and meet some need that society has—the need for international students to feel connected to their adopted culture.

The Lord has given her a love for China and the Chinese people. She has been to China three times—writing, smuggling Bibles, and most recently working with orphans and abandoned children. Three years ago she co-authored a book on China entitled, *China: The Hidden Miracle.*

As part of her love for other nations, she has worked closely with international students and organizations that minister to them. While she lived in Alabama, she served as president of the Mobile Council for International Friendship, a group of city churches that reached out to international students in "friendship evangelism." She served as editor for *The Mandate*, a newspaper that reaches out to the 40,000 Chinese students studying in the U.S. This was a non-paying position, and she raised her own support for this job. Today, she is developing a computer network for everyone working with international students.

Her life verse is found in Revelation 7:9:

There I saw a great multitude from every race, every nation, and tribe, wearing royal robes of righteousness washed white by the blood of the Lamb. Day and night they are standing there waving palm branches in their hands, saying 'Salvation belongs to our God who sits on the throne and to the Lamb.'

If that is what heaven will be like, she believes the Church on earth should be no different, and she is committed to reaching out to people of other cultures and nations.

God has taken her life-long love and fascination for travel and international people and places, and shown her how to practically serve people.

What about you? Whom are you serving? What group of people are enjoying the gifts and purpose that God has invested in you? Are you just working to live and earn money, or does your job and daily routine fit into some societal need?

Chapter Six

Purpose Brings Pleasure

The return from your work must be the satisfaction which that work brings you and the world's need of that work. With this, life is heaven, or as near as heaven as you can get. Without this—with work which you despise, which bores you, and which the world does not need—this life is hell.

—William Du Bois

I love planning conferences and special events. When I see people arriving at an event that I've planned, I get a rush of joy that's hard to describe. I don't even have to sit in the sessions or listen to the speakers to appreciate the conference. Seeing the results of my work when people come and enjoy themselves is joy enough for me. And as soon as the event is over, no matter how hard I've worked or how well it's gone (or hasn't gone), I'm always ready to do another one.

There's no way to explain this joyful feeling apart from how it relates to my purpose. My purpose is to bring order out of chaos. I love taking a concept for a meeting, talking it through so that everyone understands what the "end product" should look like, and then bringing something (a program, the budget, facilities, brochure, and finally the event) out of nothing—out of an idea. My purpose isn't to organize conferences, but my purpose of bringing order out of chaos is expressed in that activity. And it brings me great joy.

We've already looked briefly at the connection between joy and purpose in Chapter Three. But this critical issue deserves further discussion. I've found that joy is the primary indicator when someone—anyone—is functioning in or around their life purpose. It's that simple, but many try to make it harder than that.

The concept of joy in fulfilling your purpose can be a tricky one. For many, pleasure isn't a good indicator of what they were born to do. Some feel that pleasure is too easily sidetracked into selfish pursuits that are often contrary to the will of God. Others just don't trust their pleasure "barometer"; if it feels good, it can't be good, no matter how good or righteous it may seem to be. Or they at least feel that pleasure shouldn't be the motivating factor for doing much of anything.

At one seminar I was conducting, one pianist told me, "I loved playing the piano so much that I gave it up." I was incredulous and found out that this person was doing something that she only tolerated now, rather than pursuing the activity she loved. But this person's mindset was that her enjoyment *could* make her piano playing an activity that *could* take the place of God in her life; it *could* become an idolatrous thing.

So rather than take the risk of messing up what she loved doing, she gave it up to pursue a job she didn't enjoy, but that paid her some money. What kind of God would give her a love for playing the piano and then ask her to walk away from it for the rest of her life? That is a concept I'll never understand, but I do understand the root of that thinking.

Joy is an indicator of what it is that God made you to do and be. Man has abused the concept of pleasure, but that doesn't mean that pleasure is an issue to be avoided at all costs. You don't refrain from driving over a bridge just because it could collapse while you're on it.

Neither should you avoid doing something just because it brings you happiness and joy. You were created to enjoy your work, and that's something that God built into man's being. Man's "pleasure meter," so to speak, was to register high marks when man served the Lord and entered into His joy.

My friend, Jim Newsom, whom I mentioned earlier, does an anti-drug presentation in schools. In this presentation, Jim doesn't only say that drugs are bad. He truthfully tells the students that drugs *do* bring pleasure; they do make you feel good! So he wins the attention of any young person who has experimented with drugs, because they *know* that drugs make you feel good; they bring you temporary pleasure; they register on your pleasure meter.

Jim goes on to say, however, that drugs eventually take something, and what they take in the long run isn't worth what they give in the short run. Jim speaks from personal experience, since a life of drug abuse led him to take the life of another human being. His presentation is so powerful and convincing that many young people turn in their drug paraphernalia when the presentation is over.

And Jim's presentation is consistent with the

Bible. The writer of Hebrews wrote that Moses chose not "to enjoy the pleasures of sin for a short time" (Hebrews 11:25). Doing something wrong can feel good. Contrast this notion of pleasure as immediate gratification with the chief end of man as described in the *Westminster Catechism,* "The chief end of man is to glorify God and enjoy Him forever." There's joy in knowing and serving God—that's part of the human experience as designed by God. And your purpose is where that enjoyment is best experienced. Joy can be a pursuit in itself, and that can make it dangerous or at least frivolous. Joy, as a by-product of doing the work you love, is to be expected.

In *Desiring God: Meditations of a Christian Hedonist,* John Piper writes,

> Christian Hedonism is a philosophy of life built on the following five convictions:
>
> 1. The longing to be happy is a universal human experience, and it is good, not sinful.
>
> 2. We should never try to deny or resist our longing to be happy, as though it was a bad impulse. Instead we should seek to intensify this longing and

nourish it with whatever will provide the deepest and most enduring satisfaction.

3. The deepest and most enduring happiness is found only in God. Not from God, but in God.

4. The happiness we find in God reaches its consummation when it is shared with others in the manifold ways of love.

5. To the extent we try to abandon the pursuit of our own pleasure, we fail to honor God and love people. Or, to put it positively: the pursuit of pleasure is a necessary part of all worship and virtue. That is,

The chief end of man is to glorify God
BY
enjoying him forever.

King Solomon wrote,

So I saw that there is nothing better for a man than to enjoy his work, because that is his lot (Ecclesiastes 3:22).

Then I realized that it is good and proper for a man to eat and drink, and to find satisfaction in his toilsome labor under the sun during the few days of life God has given him—for this is his lot (Ecclesiastes 5:18).

If Solomon summarized his lifelong pursuit of wisdom with these statements, don't you think that what you enjoy doing is at least some indication of your life's purpose? Laurence Boldt writes:

> That is what is meant by finding a life's work, by doing the work you love. It is not necessarily that it is always easy or even always pleasurable. On the contrary, true love has the element of sacrifice, a readiness to suffer for something greater than oneself. Yet, as Samuel Johnson put it, "He that labors in any great or laudable undertaking has his fatigues first supported by hope, and afterwards rewarded by joy."

What does that mean for you as you pursue your purpose? What do you do that makes you feel peaceful and maybe even exhilarated? What do you dream about doing that brings you a sense that if you really did do it, you would be happy? Is it travel? Starting a business? A ministry? Giving away large sums of money? Singing before a large audience? Writing a book?

I'm amazed at how many people feel stuck

in what they're doing, and often it takes a life crisis of some kind to get them to reconsider and even change course. Are you one of them? In his book, *The Power of Purpose,* Richard Leider writes,

> As Maslov stated, "Even if all these needs [physical needs, safety and security, a sense of companionship and affection] are satisfied, we may still often (if not always) expect that a new discontent and restlessness will soon develop unless the individual is doing what he is fitted for. A musician must make music, an artist must paint, a writer must write if he is to be ultimately at peace with himself. What a man can be, he must be. This need we call self-actualization." At the highest level, we operate with purpose. At this level we are growing, stretching, and utilizing our highest gifts and talents. We have a clear answer for the question, "Why do I get up on Monday morning?" Stop for a moment and ask yourself: "Why do I get up on Monday morning?" Repeat the question several times out loud.

Why do you get up on Monday morning? Is it

to get to do that which you love doing, or is it to earn a paycheck? Where has your sense of wonder and adventure gone? Is money the thing that you seek and serve? Ralph Waldo Emerson wrote, "If you love and serve man, you cannot, by any hiding or stratagem, escape remuneration." Are you willing to take steps to recapture your joy, and better yet, to let your joy guide you to where you need to be?

Whatever your life purpose is, don't ignore it because you're afraid of the joy it might bring. Use the joy as an indicator that what you're considering, or actually doing, is bringing joy because it's God's will for you. And that joy can be a regular companion, not an occasional visitor, if you'll only operate in your purpose more often.

As Boldt wrote, "It [your life's purpose] is not necessarily that it is always easy or even always pleasurable." Joy comes to help you through the difficulties that inevitably come with life and work.

Chapter Seven

Purpose Brings Pain

*Do not lose heart even if you must wait
a bit before finding the right thing. Be
prepared for disappointment, also! But
do not abandon the quest.*
        —Albert Schweitzer

A man named Saul, who later became
known as the Apostle Paul, encountered his purpose one day on a road leading to Damascus. He
called it a light from heaven. Purpose doesn't
come from personal enlightenment or from self-
discovery: purpose is a *revelation*. Consider
Saul's experience:

> *On one of these journeys I was going to
> Damascus with the authority and com-
> mission of the chief priests. About noon,
> O king, as I was on the road,* I saw a
> light from heaven, brighter than the sun,
> blazing around me and my companions.

We all fell to the ground, and I heard a voice saying to me in Aramaic . . . So then, King Agrippa, I was not disobedient to the vision from heaven (Acts 26:12-14,19, emphasis added).

This man Saul walked away from that road and went down another road, the road called purpose. That road brought him much success and fulfillment, but it also brought him a lot of hard work and pain. And it also was his entrance to the hereafter. He saw a light from heaven and cooperated with the purpose God had for him. He lived another 30 years, planted a number of churches, wrote letters or epistles to those churches, and then was martyred for his faith in the God of his purpose. He still speaks to those who will listen out of the power of his purpose.

And listen to what he says to us today:

I have worked much harder, been in prison more frequently, been flogged more severely, and been exposed to death again and again. Five times, I received from the Jews the forty lashes minus one. Three times I was beaten with rods, once I was stoned, three times I was ship-wrecked, I spent a night and a day in the open sea, I have been constantly on the

> *move, I have been in danger from rivers, in danger from bandits, in danger from my own countrymen, in danger from Gentiles; in danger in the city, in danger in the country, in danger at sea; and in danger from false brothers. I have labored and toiled and have often gone without sleep; I have known hunger and thirst and have often gone without food; I have been cold and naked. Besides everything else, I face daily the pressure of my concern for all the churches. Who is weak, and I do not feel weak?* (2 Corinthians 11:23-29).

Now Saul is arguably an extreme case. The nature of his pioneering work led him to face much more than most of us will ever encounter. But the principle is still true: your purpose will lead you to some painful experiences. In fact, that can be another indicator of what your purpose truly is.

Over what do you weep? What angers you consistently? If waste of resources angers you, perhaps you are to conserve and protect. If inefficiency frustrates you, maybe you are to be a model of efficiency, finding efficient ways to do old or new things. If you recognize that people are not being utilized properly at work or in the church, possibly you are to help find strategies of how to best utilize human resources.

While purpose exhilarates you and allows you to "feel God's pleasure," it also opens up a world of need that can be overwhelming. You feel the pain of others, and sometimes of God, for a broken and fallen world. Your purpose gives you a heightened awareness to certain problems, and you can't get away from the burden to get involved. Remember, God so loved people that He sent someone. God wants to send *you* into a world that desperately needs you and what you have to offer.

I am convinced that the price keeps some of us from seeking or fulfilling purpose. You may know the cost that awaits you and intuitively seek safer ground in busywork, family, or church life. It can be a difficult job identifying your purpose, but even more difficult carrying it out. That can keep you from seriously searching, so that you remain content with a vague definition.

Geoffrey M. Bellman writes in *Your Signature Path,*

One definition of passion is an "intense, driving, or overmastering feeling or

73

conviction." How does this definition fit with your feelings about your work? What powerful or compelling emotions do you experience in the pursuit of your work? Another definition is "strong amorous feeling; love." Test that against what you feel at work. The word *passion* comes from the Latin *pati,* to suffer or submit. How does that fit? Notice the feelings passion arouses in us as it pulls on our emotions, or arouses us, or causes us to suffer. All of these definitions together express an array of feelings that can be associated with the passionate path of work—work as powerful emotion, submission, and suffering. These interwoven themes snake along the work path, bringing agony, ecstasy, and meaning.

Work and passion are seldom considered together. Anger and passion? Yes. Sex and passion? Certainly. Politics and passion? Okay. But work and passion? This chapter searches for the passion we bring to our work, the ways we pursue it, and the ways we express it. It is about the potentially compelling, passionate relationship between work and the worker. We often speak of work as a burden that is laid on us by others, as if we had no choice in taking on the burden. Listen to yourself; listen to others.

My passion to bring order out of chaos has made me a busy man. I'm administrator for a large, local church and oversee my pastor's calendar (he travels 225 days annually). I'm also the director for an international network of churches—that alone takes me out of the country four to six times per year. I'm trying to mentor several young, emerging leaders in my church-setting, and I travel, giving seminars. I consult with local churches and church networks to help them bring order out of their chaos. I also write and speak in church and non-church settings.

Years ago I was complaining to the Lord that I was too busy and under too much pressure. I began a two-week "search" to identify areas that I could eliminate from my schedule and world. Then one morning I awoke with a particular verse from the Bible on my mind. I went to my Bible, and this is what I read:

But by the grace of God I am what I am, but his grace to me was not without effect. No, I worked harder than all of them—yet not I, but the grace of God that was with me (1 Corinthians 15:10).

My search ended with the realization that my purpose—order out of chaos—was going to require not just what I was giving, but more if I was to fulfill it adequately.

I saw then that hard work "came with the territory." And not all my hard work has been rewarded with the order I was trying to bring. My own mistakes, the fears of those in charge, people who preferred the status quo, and some measure of spiritual opposition have led me to discouragement, depression, financially lean times, and even unemployment! I have stayed up nights, traveled 1.5 million miles as of the writing of this book, and prayed long and hard for answers and insight, some of which have not yet arrived.

And I've talked with others who have discovered their purpose and found that their stories are the same: Exhilaration in finding purpose, but occasional pain in expressing it. Yet there's no other road to travel, no other lifestyle to embrace. For purpose is my due north compass point, keeping me on course and effective. I refuse to stop bringing order because it may lead to some tough times and work.

Then there's also the pain of imperfection that is part of this world. I know that I am and will continue to be human, and part of the human experience is learning from mistakes and trial-and-error. But I am reminded of the words of Henry Wordsworth Longfellow:

> The heights by great men reached and kept
> Were not attained by sudden flight.
> But they, while their companions slept,
> Were toiling upward in the night.

I want to keep working and growing in spite of my mistakes. I want to keep reaching upward for a meaningful life as defined by God's will for me. I refuse to give up my life's agenda in response to my own failures or to the uncertainty of life.

How about you? Will you stay in your comfort zone because you're afraid of pain? How long will you settle for being cooped up in a lifestyle that has no purpose or fulfillment? Or, with faith, resolve and courage, will you finally venture out into a world of purpose that can bring discomfort but also joys unspeakable?

I've made up my mind. I'll not settle for anything less. I've tasted the ecstasy of purpose and there's no turning back. For instance, I *know* that Africa looms large in my future because there's a lot of chaos there to which God wants me to bring order. I have a consulting and conference planning business in my future that will take ideas and make them a profitable reality. There are many people who agree with the truth of purpose, but can't seem to grasp hold of the specific reality for themselves. I want to speak to as many of those as I can before I depart this life. And I want to leave a written legacy of books and devotionals that will speak to others after I'm gone.

But there's one final pain connected with purpose. For some, it is the difficulty in *finding* it. You may still say after reading these pages, "I have no idea what my purpose is." To you I can only say, "Don't give up."

The famous poet, ee cummings, once wrote,

> It takes the courage to be nobody-but-yourself—in a world which is doing its best, night and day, to make you everybody else, [and that] means to fight the hardest battle which any human being can fight; and never stop fighting.

It's a battle for some to discover that nugget of purpose, for it's sometimes buried under generations of rubble and failure.

Your journey may include a string of jobs and experiences that have not defined what your purpose is, but what it is NOT. You may have eagerly set out on a course that you were certain was your purpose course, only to have had to backtrack to the beginning to start over again.

Why this pain? Why do some have a Damascus-road-experience like Saul, while others seem to labor in obscurity, asking questions for which no answers seem to come? The only answer can be in what I call the enhanced-appreciation concept. Let me explain.

When I go to a symphony orchestra concert, I enjoy the music. But I will never enjoy it like people who have studied music all their life, who have spent countless hours practicing their craft, or who have spent days in rehearsals hammering out a good sound with dozens of others striving for the same thing. A person who has been through more than I to get to that concert has an enhanced appreciation of the final product, an appreciation that I can never enter into.

And so it will be with you. Your extra digging, searching, and false starts will only enhance your appreciation for the real thing. And you'll certainly never settle for anything less once you've found the real thing. You won't waste a single minute on being anything you're *not* after you've spent your life finding out who you *are*. There is a pain in paying the price to discover your purpose that can only bring great relief when you find what it is.

I recently visited a 62-year-old missionary friend in South Africa. He has been there for 10 years and has little to show for it. His ministry in the United States prior to that was less than successful. Out of frustration, last year he took a position with a Bible College needing help. Today he is responsible for a complete turnaround in that institution.

While having dinner with him, he said to me, "John, I finally figured it out—what I'm supposed to do with my life. It makes so much sense now, and has helped me make sense of my past as well. I just don't know now how many years I have to finish the job."

None of us know how many years we have, but my friend can finish his days in a place of fruitful labor that is bringing him joy and pain. He didn't give up in his quest, and he was rewarded with his purpose. I encourage you to do the same.

So, let's review. You now know that:
• Productivity is a priority.
• Productivity requires purpose.

- Purpose is personal and progressive.
- Purpose demands proof.
- Purpose is practical.
- Purpose brings pleasure.
- Purpose brings pain.

Armed with this knowledge, work through the case studies and examples contained throughout this book. Obtain the audio cassette and listen to it again and again. Look at the bibliography and choose another title or titles to read that will help you become clearer about your purpose and life's work.

Remember, *"God makes everything for His own purpose, even the wicked for the day of evil"* (Proverbs 16:4). With that in mind, don't settle for anything less than total life focus.

For Additional Information

If I can help you, don't hesitate to write me at:
P.O. Box 91069
Pittsburgh, PA 15221

or, e-mail me at:
JohnStanko@att.net

or, for more material to help you find
your purpose, visit my website at:
www.purposequest.com

Also, feel free to send me your own purpose story or journey. It may find its way into a future publication and be used to help other purpose pilgrims.

Please contact the publisher
to order my other books:
Evergreen Press
P.O. Box 191540
Mobile, AL 36619
800-367-8203

Appendix I

Vocation and Calling

The following are some helpful quotes and thoughts in terminology and perspective that might be helpful in thinking about purpose:

• Where your talents and the needs of the world cross, there lies your vocation.
—Aristotle

• A man knows he has found his vocation when he stops thinking about how to live and begins to live.
—Thomas Merton

• Within a few months of this time of consecration [his conversion to Christianity] the impression was wrought into my soul that it was in China the Lord wanted me. It seemed to me highly probably that the work to which I was then called might cost my life.
—J. Hudson Taylor, *Autobiography* (Minneapolis: Bethany House, p.15).

• There are three words that tend to be used interchangeably—and shouldn't be. They are "vocation," "career" and "job." Vocation is the most profound of the three, and it has to do with your calling. It's what you're doing in life that makes a difference for you, that builds meaning for you, that you can look back on in your later years to see the impact you've made on the world. A calling is something you have to listen for. You don't hear it once and then immediately recognize it. You've got to attune yourself to the message.

Career is the term you hear most often today. A career is a line of work. You can say that your career is to be a lawyer or a securities analyst—but usually it's not the same as your calling. You can have different careers at different points in your life.

A *job* is the most specific and immediate of the three terms. It has to do with who's employing you at the moment and what your job description is for the next 6 months or so.
—Timothy Butler, director for MBA career development programs at Harvard University Business School
• If you look at the derivations of the words *"career"* and *"vocation,"* you immediately get a feel for the difference between them. Vocation comes from the

Latin *vocare,* which means "to call." It suggests that you are listening for something that calls out to you, something that comes to you and is particular to you. "Career" comes originally from the Latin word for "cart", and later from the Middle French word for "race track." In other words, you go around and around really fast for a long-time—but you never get there.
—James Waldroop, director of MBA career development programs at Harvard University Business School

• Your job and career can and probably will change over time. Your purpose never will.
—John Stanko

• Blessed is the man who has found his work. Let him ask no other blessing.
—Thomas Carlyle

Can you distinguish between your calling or purpose and your career? My calling or purpose is to bring order out of chaos. My career is church administration. My job at this writing is Administrative Pastor at Covenant Church of Pittsburgh. How about you? What calls out to you, like chaos calls out to me? Fill in the blanks below.

My calling or vocation is _____
_____
_____
_____.

My career is _____
_____
_____
_____.

Right now, my job is _____
_____
_____
_____.

Appendix II
A Formula for a Lifestyle Rich in Purpose

Repacking your Bags
by Richard J. Leider and David A. Shapiro

(Talent + Passions + Environment) x Vision = *Lifestyle Rich in Purpose*

A " lifestyle rich in purpose" is the sum of:

• Your talents:
___ Skills that you truly enjoy expressing
___ Abilities that come naturally, effortlessly, and spontaneously
___ Abilities you can't remember learning because you've been doing them effortlessly for so long

• Your passion:
___ Problems you strongly feel need solving in the world

___ Issues in which you'd love to be more involved

___ Areas you obsess about or would like to learn more about

___ Activities which reflect deep and consistent interests

• Your preferred environment:

___ The ideal work environment that would make it easiest or most comfortable for you to express your true talents and passions

___ Place and style preferences (Most people get hired, fired, promoted, demoted, or find satisfaction based on their ability to align themselves with their environment.)

• Your vision:

___ How do you see yourself putting it all together?

___ How do you envision the hoped-for future, and how is what you're doing now getting you there?

___ What does succeeding in the next year or more look like?

Respond to these categories as best you can and see what emerges. Are you any closer to defining your life's purpose? I hope so!

Appendix III

A Closer Look at What We Know About the Apostle Paul, a Man of Purpose

Paul made tents for a living, but he never saw himself as a "tent maker." What did he have to say about his purpose? In every epistle he wrote, he referred to what he had been born to do and *never* did he write that it was to make tents. He was clear enough to talk about his purpose every chance he had.

- Romans 1:5,13,16
- Romans 15:7-29
- 1 Corinthians 1:17,24
- 1 Corinthians 3:5-15
- 2 Corinthians 5:16-21
- 2 Corinthians 10:12-18
- Galatians 1:15-16

- Galatians 2:2,7-9
- Ephesians 3:1-10,7-12
- Philippians 1:12-18
- Colossians 1:27-29
- 1 Thessalonians 1:4-5
- 1 Thessalonians 2:16
- 2 Thessalonians 3:1-4
- 1 Timothy 2:5-7
- 2 Timothy 4:17
- Titus 1:1-3

SPECIAL NOTE: If you know your Bible, you'll say, "Hey, wait a minute! Paul wrote 13 epistles and there are only 12 listed above. I thought you said he referred to his purpose in all 13?"

Well, I did write that—and it's true. While Paul did not specifically mention his purpose in his epistle to Philemon, he was writing about an escaped slave who was now a Christian. The whole letter addresses a problem that was unique to the Gentile world, which was Paul's sphere of ministry.

The book of Acts, which chronicles life and ministry in the early church, spends a great deal of time relating stories of Saul (Paul) and his purpose.

- Acts 9:15
- Acts 13:1-4
- Acts 13:47
- Acts 14:27
- Acts 15:3,7
- Acts 21:11,19-21
- Acts 20:24
- Acts 22:14-21
- Acts 26:16-19

On six separate occasions, Paul had a vision or supernatural visitation. It is of interest that on each occasion, the visitation was to reveal or encourage him in his purpose.

- Acts 9:1-9
- Acts 16:9-10
- Acts 18:9-11
- Acts 22:17
- Acts 23:11
- Acts 27:24

Appendix IV

Repacking Your Bags: Lighten Your Load for the Rest of Your Life

by Richard J. Leider/ David A. Shapiro

In the above-mentioned book, the authors try to help the reader to find the right balance between the conflicting priorities in life. To do this, they point out that each of us carries three bags through the trip of life. They are:

1) A briefcase—work baggage
2) An overnight bag—your love baggage
3) A trunk—your place baggage

With this in mind, they then pose numerous questions for the reader to answer that will help you "unpack" bags and then to repack them with items you most definitely want to carry. Their questions may help you find answers as you seek to unpack and repack your purpose bag.

"What Do You Do?"

Unpacking Your Briefcase

- What are your hidden talents? How does your work give you the opportunity to express those talents?
- What do you think "needs doing" in today's world? How does your work allow you to make a contribution to that?
- What is your ideal work environment? How does your current work environment compare?
- Who do you want to serve in your work? How does your current work involve you with those people?
- Picture your typical work day. What is it filled with? How much of "you" goes through the door, and how much of "you" do you check at the entrance?
- Imagine your ideal work associates. How do your current work associates stack up?
- Does your work make you happy?

"Who Do You Love?"

Unpacking Your Overnight Bag

- Who are the people you feel closest to in your life and why?

- What do you miss most when the people you care about most are away?
- What life dreams do you share with the people you're closest to?
- Describe a typical day spent with those you love best. What's the best part of the day?
- How did you meet those you're closest to? What drew you to them first?
- Do you spend as much time as you like with your loved ones? How could you spend more?
- How do you want to be remembered by those you love?
- Does you relationship life make you happy?

"Is There No Place Like Home?"

Unpacking Your Trunk

- When you think of "home," what images spring to mind?
- What are the qualities that make "home" home to you?
- What is your most prized possession? If your home was burning down, what would you grab?
- When you look around your home, what makes you happy? What feels like clutter?

- What about your sense of community? Do you feel like you belong? How are you contributing?
- If you could live anywhere, where would it be? Why aren't you living there now?
- Does your home and living environment make you happy?

Do your answers reveal any clues or patterns to what your purpose could be, or where and with whom you can fulfill it?

Appendix V

The Path: Creating Your Mission Statement

by Laurie Beth Jones

In her classic book, *The Path,* Laurie Jones makes a case for having both a life vision and mission statement. She writes, "While a mission statement is centered around the process of what you need to be doing, a vision statement is the end result of what you will have done." With this distinction in mind, she asks 19 questions that may be helpful to you as you search for your life's purpose and how you will carry it out. Jones writes,

> When you are writing out your vision statement, think about a world where, "With God, anything is possible." Color outside the lines. Look at people who are having, being, doing, creating what you want to create as role models.

Exercise

Questions for Individuals

1. Who is living the life you most envy?
2. Describe what you think it is like.
3. Who is doing the kind of work you most wish you could be doing?
4. Describe what their work life must be like.
5. If you only had six healthy months left to live, what would they look like?
6. What do you want more of:
    - in your relationships
    - in your work
7. What do you want less of:
    - in your relationships
    - in your work
8. Describe in detail your ideal work setting.
9. Describe in detail your ideal work day.
10. Describe in detail your ideal co-workers.
11. If money were no object, what would you be doing with your life?
12. What would you do if you were ten times bolder?
    - In your primary love relationships?
    - In your work setting?
    - In your community?
    - In your family?

- In your place of worship?

13. Imagine that it is Monday morning, 9 A.M., three years from now.
    - Where are you?
    - What are you doing?
    - Who are you seeing?
    - What are you wearing?

14. It is now noon, same day.
    - Who are you going to see?
    - Where are you going for lunch?

15. It is now Saturday, 6 P.M.
    - Where are you?
    - What are you doing?
    - Who are you seeing?
    - What are you wearing?

16. You are now a very old person, walking with a school child who asks you, "What are you most proud of about your life?"

17. You are about to die. What did you accomplish before you left?

18. As a result of your having lived, three things have changed or shifted in the world. What are they?

19. Now write out your vision statement, incorporating your responses from all of the questions above.

Appendix VI

Jesus—The Same

As you read this excerpt from *Jesus—the Same,* author unknown (published by Discipleship Publications International, One Merril Street, Woburn, MA 01801), I trust that you will be impressed that your purpose, which "narrows" your world, opens the entire world to you at the same time. A paradox? An oxymoron? Read on.

The Narrowness of Jesus

Let us think about the narrowness of Jesus. He set definite boundaries for himself; he shut himself up within contracted limitations, and in this sense he was narrow. How narrow was the circle inside of which he did all his work? He lived his life in Palestine, a little country no larger than Connecticut. It was not a prominent country either, but only a little province tributary to mighty Rome. It had no figure in the eye of the world.

He might have traveled across the world as many illustrious teachers had done before his day. He might have taught in Athens and lifted up his voice in the streets of Rome, the eternal city. He might have given His message to a wide circle of men whose influence covered many lands; but he rather chose to stay at home to give his time to the cities of Galilee, to pour out his strength on the villages of Judea. For 30 years, he remained in the dingy obscurity of a carpenter's shop, and the country upon which he poured out the full wealth of his brains and heart was only a carpenter's shop among the palaces of the earth.

If his field was contracted, so also was the character of his work: He only tried to do one thing. There were 1,000 good things which a good man in Palestine might have done, but he left 999 of them unattempted and confined himself to the one thing which he believed his heavenly father had given him to do. Men do not understand such narrowness. They were always urging him to swing into a wider orbit, into the something which would create a greater stir. A man one day interrupted him while he was speaking, saying, "Make my brother divide the inheritance with me." But his reply was, "That lies outside my province. Come in and listen to me, and I would do for you the service which God has appointed me to do." It was a righteous piece of work that the man wanted to have done; but it was not Christ's work, and therefore He would not do it. No one man can do everything. There are a thousand things which need to be done, yet which no man, however industrious and noble, can perform. Jesus set limits to his activity, and beyond those limits, no man ever persuaded Him to go.

One day his brothers wanted him to go to Jerusalem and make an impression on the big men there, but He refused to listen to their exhortation, telling them that they might go anytime they choose, but that it was different with Him. He could not go until it was time for Him to go—until his work compelled him to go. He could not go until His hour had come. When the hour arrived, He set His face steadfastly to go to Jerusalem. All along the way, men tried to divert him, but He could not be dissuaded. To Jerusalem He must go. It was for Him to walk along the narrow path, for this alone led to the glorious life which was to cheer and save the world. When He talks to men about the two ways—one of them narrow and the other one broad—He's speaking out of His own experience, and when He urges men to choose the narrow one in preference to the one that is broad, He is only saying, "Follow Me."

It is only when a man picks out some particular little sphere and says, "Inside of this, I purpose to work," that real life begins and his heart learns the art of singing. So long as the world's work lies in a mountain mass, there is only depression and a hopelessness; it is when a man picks up in his hand a definite, tiny task and says, "This is the thing to which I shall devote my life," that the shadows vanish and life becomes worth living. It is that narrow path that leads to life.

Jesus' work was definite. At 12, He knew the business to which He must give Himself. There never was a day in which He allowed Himself to be moved into doing something else. Right here is where we are prone to blunder, and it is at this point that we should look for the root cause of much of the disquiet in our souls. We start out to do a certain work, and immediately people begin to say, "Why don't you do this?" "Come and do this." And before we are aware of our folly, we have dissipated our energy in trying to do things which God never intended us to attempt. It is here that we blunder in our benevolence. We tried to give to too many causes, and the result is we have little joy in our giving. It is no man's duty to contribute to every good cause that passes his way, and it is only when we draw a circle around our generosity that we become what God likes to see—a cheerful giver. If you want to see a man who sings at his work, look for him inside a narrow circle.

Focused light has tremendous power. Diffused light has no power at all. For instance, by focusing the power of the sun through a magnifying glass, you can set a leaf on fire. But you can't set a leaf on fire if the same sunlight is unfocused. When light is concentrated at an even higher level—like a laser beam—it can even cut through a block of steel.

The principle of concentration works in other areas, too. The focused life and focused churches will have far greater impact than unfocused ones. Like a laser beam, the more focused your church becomes, the more impact it will have on society. Paul said, *"I am bringing all my energies to bear on this one thing, forgetting what is behind and looking forward to what lies ahead"* (Philippians 3:13, Living Bible). If the energy of the church is diffused and dissipated, the power is lost.

Not only was Jesus joyful, but He was mighty. He made an impression because He stayed in one place and hit the same nail on the head until it was driven completely in. Had He wandered over the earth speaking His parables, they would have fallen into more ears but would have molded fewer hearts. By staying in Palestine and keeping His heart close to a few chosen hearts, He became increasingly influential, so much so that the authorities became frightened, fearing that He may overturn the nation. The men who were the nearest to Him became so passionately in love with Him that they were ready to die for Him. He made Himself mighty by limiting Himself.

What is it to succeed? It is to do the thing for which we were created. The most galling of all experiences is the failure to do that which is most worthwhile. Jesus attempted to do one thing only, and that was to perform the work which His Father had given Him to do. At the end of His life, He could look into His Father's face and say, "I have finished the work that You gave me to do."

The Breadth of Jesus

He had apparently no desire to see the world, and intended to spend His life in little Palestine. He walked a path that was narrow, and refused to give His approval to men and measures that won the esteem and praise of thousands of His countrymen. But there was a purpose in this narrowness and a reason for it. His narrowness was a product of his breadth.

He walked the narrow path because He carried in His heart the dream of an empire which was vast. By standing in one place and striking repeatedly the strings of the same set of hearts, He started vibrations that have filled the world with music. By carefully tending the fire that He had kindled, He made it hot enough to change the spiritual climate of many lands. By saturating a little circle of chosen followers with His Spirit, He made them capable of carrying on their shoulders a lost race to God. By persistently treading a single path, He made that path so luminous that every eye could see it.

By being faithful in a few things, He won the place of Lordship over many cities; and in limiting Himself of no reputation, He founded a kingdom broad as humanity and of which there should be no end.

At an early stage, He told his apostles not to go outside the limits of their own people in their work; but this limitation of field was only educational, and with their increasing strength, was to pass forever away. Men should stay in Jerusalem long enough to secure strength sufficient to grapple with problems of Judea; and they should tarry in Judea until they are capable of grappling with the more difficult conditions of Samaria; and they should work in Samaria until they have acquired the endurance which would enable them to travel to the uttermost parts of the earth.

Appendix VII
Providential Perspective

The following article is adapted from the newsletter entitled *Providential Perspective,* the teaching journal of The Providence Foundation (Vol.10, No.5, November 1995). Stephen McDowell wrote the newsletter article. It includes material from *Almighty Sons: Doing Business God's Way,* by Dennis Peacocke, and *Cyrus Hall McCormick: His Life and Work,* by Herbert N. Casson.

McDowell writes,

> He [Jesus] told us to "do business with this until I come back" (Luke 19:13). The *this* are minas, which certainly speak of wise money usage, but in a broader sense represent the talents, skills, and abilities God has given each of us. God created us for a purpose (Genesis 1:26-28). He wants us to work

as partners with Him to take dominion over the earth by using the talents He has given us. These talents express themselves in the business or work He has called us to perform. Our work is a vital part of God's plan for us and the nations. As we are faithful to labor hard and multiply what He has given us, we will be taking part in bringing forth His Kingdom on earth and being a blessing to the nations.

Cyrus McCormick was a faithful servant who utilized the talents God gave him, and in so doing elevated the position of farmers and common laborers, helped provide abundant and affordable bread to the nations, and lay the foundation for the advancement and prosperity of America and many other nations. He fulfilled his Kingdom purpose.

Biblical Principles of Business and Work Exemplified in Cyrus' Life

1) Work is a holy calling. We should love it and work hard.
2) Business is a means of serving and blessing others. His business innovations that served and blessed included:

- A written guarantee
- Grain reapers sold at a known price
- Gaining the customer's good will through credit terms for machinery and service repairs and spare parts availability, both revolutionary concepts in their day.

3) Business must be built on integrity and godly principles.

4) Business growth comes from encouraging individual initiative and seeing that all involved benefit from the fruit of their labor.

5) Incorporating the family into your business is a means of building wealth generationally.

You do not have to be like Cyrus McCormick and invent something great to fulfill your divine mission. But as you are providing mankind with necessary goods or services, and are helping to order and maintain God's creation, that is sacred work. This type of work can be done as a farmer, teacher, parent, manufacturer, carpenter, doctor, store clerk, etc.

How about you? What is your sacred work? Who knows? Maybe you will change the world like Cyrus McCormick did—by finding and carrying out your life's purpose.

Appendix VIII
Suggested Reading

The following are books that I have read and reviewed as I have studied the purpose message. I do not endorse every idea or philosophy found in them. But I've found that each one has contributed something to my understanding of the subject, some more than others. I present these to you in the hopes that something you read in this book will cause you to dig deeper and read one or more of the books listed below.

Addington, Dr. Thomas & Grave, Dr. Stephen. *A Case for Calling.* Fayetteville, AK: Cornerstone Alliance, 1997.

Bellman, Geoffrey M. *Your Signature Path: Gaining New Perspectives on Life and Work.* San Francisco, CA: Berrett-Koehler, 1996.

Boldt, Laurence G. *How to Find the Work You Love.* New York, NY: Penguin Arkana, 1996.

Bolles, Richard Nelson. *The 1997 What Color Is Your Parachute?* Berkeley, CA: Ten Speed Press, 1996.

Braham, Barbara J. *Finding Your Purpose: A Guide to Personal Fulfillment.* Menlo Park: Crisp Publications, 1991.

Edwards, Paul and Sarah. *Finding Your Perfect Work.* New York: G.P. Putnam's Sons, 1996.

Finney, Martha & Dasch, Deborah. *Find Your Calling, Love Your Life.* New York: Simon & Schuster, 1998.

Handy, Charles. *The Age of Unreason.* Boston: Harvard Business School Press, 1990.

Jones, Laurie Beth. *The Path: Creating Your Mission Statement.* New York: Hyperion, 1996.

Leider, Richard J. & Shapiro, David A. *Repacking Your Bags: Lighten Your Load for the Rest of Your Life.* San Francisco, CA: Berrett-Koehler, 1996.

Leider, Richard J. *The Power of Purpose: Creating Meaning in Your Life and Work.* San Francisco, CA: Berrett-Koehler, 1997.

McCarthy, Kevin W. *The On-Purpose Person: Making Your Life Make Sense.* Colorado Springs, CO: Pinon Press, 1992.

McPherson, Nenien C., Jr. *The Power of a Purpose.* New York: Revell, 1959.

Peacocke, Dennis. *Almighty Sons: Doing Business God's Way!* Santa Rosa, CA: Rebuild, 1995.

Piper, John. *Desiring God: Meditations of a Christian Hedonist.* Sisters, OR: Multnomah, 1996.

Sinetar, Marsha. *Do What You Love, The Money Will Follow.* New York, NY: Dell, 1987.

Stephan, Naomi, Ph.D. *Fulfill Your Soul's Purpose: Ten Creative Paths to Your Life Mission.* Walpole, NH: Stillpoint Publishing, 1994.

Waitley, Denis. *The New Dynamics of Goal Setting.* New York, NY: Quill, 1996.

Printed in the United States
41338LVS00001B/274-375